OUTDOOR LIVING™

HIKING

AMY BEATTIE AND SARA COPPIN

ROSEN
PUBLISHING

NEW YORK

Published in 2016 by The Rosen Publishing Group, Inc.
29 East 21st Street, New York, NY 10010

Copyright © 2016 by The Rosen Publishing Group, Inc.

First Edition

Library of Congress Cataloging-in-Publication Data

Beattie, Amy.
 Hiking / Amy Beattie and Sara Coppin. -- First Edition.
    pages cm. -- ((Outdoor Living))
 Includes index.
 ISBN 978-1-4994-6231-9 (Library bound)
 1. Hiking--Juvenile literature. I. Coppin, Sara. II. Title.
 GV199.52.B43 2016
 796.51--dc23
                            2015018307

Manufactured in China

CONTENTS

INTRODUCTION

Every year, thousands of adventurers aim to hike the entire Appalachian Trail in the eastern United States. Since the trail is 2,180 miles (3,508 kilometers) long, it usually takes all spring and summer to make it from one end to the other. Hikers most often begin in the south, on Mount Springer in northern Georgia. The trail cuts through twelve more states before the final peak, Mount Katahdin, which is in central Maine.

The Appalachian Trail Conservancy estimates that only about 25 percent of the people who have attempted to hike the entire trail have succeeded. This is partly because it takes so long, but also because the trail is very challenging in some places. The section of the trail in each state is given a difficulty level from 1 to 10. The northern part of the trail requires the most rock scrambling and use of hands. Since the Appalachian Trail was completed in the late 1930s, over 15,500 people have hiked at least 2,000 miles (3,218 km) of the trail. Although most of these hikers were in their twenties, 4 percent of them were teenagers, and many older adults also completed the trail.

There are many other famous trails, peaks, and national parks to explore in North America. But you don't have to travel far or do any training to have fun hiking. Even if you live in a big city, there are probably public parks either nearby or just outside the urban area. Though there are a few safety tips to keep in mind, hiking is a fun and easy outdoor activity. All you need to do is lace up your sneakers, grab a water bottle, and head out on an adventure!

This hiker on Mount Katahdin is using her hands to help her up a steep rock face.

CHAPTER 1

THINGS TO BRING

*O*ne of the great things about hiking is that it requires very little equipment or special clothing. But especially if you're going on a day-long hike or planning to camp out for a weekend, you'll need to bring along a few things to be comfortable and stay safe while experiencing the wilderness.

ESSENTIAL ITEMS

When going out on a hike, there are a few must-have items to bring with you. First of all, you'll need a comfortable pack to carry the rest of your things. Your pack doesn't have to be huge, just big enough for one day's worth of trail supplies. It should be sturdy, comfortable, and easy to put on. A regular school backpack is fine.

The most important thing to have with you is plenty of water. Bring water from home in used spring water or juice bottles. If

It's easy to go hiking as long as you have water, a map, and other essential items with you.

you're hiking in hot weather, bring about thirty-two ounces (about one liter) of water for every two hours you are on the trail. To have cold water at midday, try freezing a few bottles the night before. As the ice melts in the hot sun, you'll have cool water to drink.

It may be tempting to drink from the freshwater streams, rivers, lakes, and ponds that you see while out on the trail, but they can make you sick. In addition to pollution caused by humans, the water may also contain many naturally occurring bacteria and other organisms such as *Cryptosporidium fungus* or *Giardia lamblia* that can cause intestinal infections and diarrhea. Many trailheads will have faucets marked "potable water," which means that the water is safe for human consumption. If there's no sign saying it's OK, don't drink the water!

Other than water, a wristwatch is probably the second most important thing to bring on your hike. Having a watch is an essential way for you to track your progress along the trail and make sure that you get back to base on time. Sunscreen and insect repellent are also crucial. That way you won't get a painful sunburn or irritating mosquito bites.

You should also bring along some snacks, particularly if you plan to be out for more than four or five hours. Hiking burns a lot of calories, and at least some of those calories must be replaced. The alternative is early exhaustion and lethargy. Simple, healthy foods such as raisins and peanuts, baked tofu, apples, cheese, jerky, and energy bars are all good hiking fare.

ITEMS TO HAVE JUST IN CASE

Hopefully you won't get lost or injured while on a hike, but in case something does happen to you, there are a few more things to have with you at all times. That way you'll be prepared if you need them.

You should plan to finish your hike long before the sun sets. But if for some reason it gets dark while you are still out on the trail, you will need to find your way out. A small but reliable flashlight will not take up much space in your pack and will give you a nice feeling of security. (Make sure you have fresh batteries.) You should also have matches or a lighter in case you need to start a fire to keep warm. Keep them in a waterproof container—they can't help if they get wet!

A good-quality folding knife or multifunction camper's tool is an indispensable item. The sharp blade is especially important for everything from cutting open a tough bag of trail mix to cutting up firewood for an emergency fire. If you purchase a folding knife, get one with a lock blade that won't accidentally close on your fingers. Another tiny item with many uses is dental floss. It could be helpful if you need to make a clothesline, replacement shoelace, sewing thread, or fishing line.

Especially if you're new to hiking, you'll probably be on familiar, well-marked trails. But getting lost is still a possibility, which is why you should always have a map of the area and a compass.

Always consult a map if you're not sure where you are or how to get where you're going.

If you have a cell phone, you may want to bring it to make a call in an emergency. However, if you're hiking in a remote area, there probably won't be any cellular service. That's why it's a good idea to carry some money with you in case you need to use a pay phone.

You may also want to have a first-aid kit in case you suffer a minor injury, such as a cut, splinter, burn, or rash. You can purchase a small travel-sized first-aid kit or put your own kit together with bandages, gauze, Band-Aids, tweezers, aspirin, antihistamines (for allergic reactions), and baking soda (which can be made into a paste and used to soothe burns and bug bites).

HENRY DAVID THOREAU

Henry David Thoreau is one of the most influential writers of American literature. Along with Ralph Waldo Emerson, he was one of the most famous followers of the literary and philosophical movement known as American Transcendentalism. Transcendentalists believed that individuals should be self-reliant because societal institutions such as churches and political parties were corrupt. They also focused on the spirituality of man and nature.

In 1845, Thoreau moved from the town of Concord, Massachusetts, to the remote area of Walden Pond, where he carefully recorded the natural history of the area. Because of his love of the outdoors and his great appreciation of the wilderness, he is sometimes called the father of the American conservation and preservation movements. In his essay entitled "Walking," Thoreau writes: "I think I cannot preserve my health and spirits, unless I spend four hours a day—and it is commonly more than that—sauntering through the woods and over the hills and fields, absolutely free from all worldly engagements."

Today Walden Pond is much busier than it was in Thoreau's time, but the state reservation caps attendance at one thousand people to make sure it doesn't get too crowded.

Finally, you may want to bring an extra pair of socks in case the pair you're wearing gets wet. Another useful clothing item is a bandanna. You can use it as a handkerchief, washcloth, towel, sweatband, pot holder, or compress.

CAMPING NECESSITIES

For many people, camping and hiking go hand in hand. There are many kinds of camping, including car or RV camping and backpacking. Backpacking means carrying all of the necessary supplies on your back and hiking into the wilderness to spend one or more nights.

If you plan to camp, you should find out what the camping rules are for the area in which you will be staying. National parks have strict rules about where and what time of year backpackers can camp and build campfires, and many campgrounds require that you make reservations for a site. The rules are established for the safety of the visitors of the park area and should not be taken lightly. One reason for these seasonal restrictions has to do with the risk of wildfires. In many wilderness areas, high summer (usually from late July through September) means dry grass and leaves. Deliberate arson, camper accidents, and even naturally occurring lightning can start deadly wildfires that can trap park visitors. In certain areas, there may be seasonal dangers caused by wildlife, such as getting too close to a mother bear and her cubs.

Camping reservations are a way for rangers to keep track of the number of people staying in the park at a given time. This information can help them to determine if and where a park visitor has gone missing. Both national parks and private campgrounds charge nightly fees.

If campfires are allowed at the campground, it's important to clean up your fire when you leave. Disperse the rocks from the fire area to more natural-looking spots, placing the burned side down. Pick up any litter and carry it out with you. Break up or cover the burned ground with dirt or gravel. If you're hiking in an area where campfires are now illegal and you see an old fire ring or site, dismantle it, too.

Once you know the rules of the area where you plan to backpack and camp, the next step is to get a map of the area and collect

To start a campfire, build a pyramid of twigs and brush that will act as kindling for larger sticks.

the necessary supplies for an overnight adventure. In addition to the items already discussed, here are the basic camping necessities:

- A large backpack. One that has a semiflexible frame, to help the pack keep its shape when full, is a good choice. Make sure that the pack is comfortable to carry even when heavy by trying it on with weights in it before heading out on the trail.
- A tent. Backpacking tents are incredibly light and fairly easy to assemble, but always make sure that you have assembled your particular tent once or twice before you go camping.
- A ground cloth. This plastic sheet goes on the ground before the tent is put up and protects the bottom of the tent from punctures, rain, snow, and dirt. Many tents have a sewn-in ground cloth.
- A sleeping bag. This should be a lightweight and easily compacted bag with either synthetic or down fill.
- A sleeping pad. It need only be as long as your torso to provide enough padding for you to sleep comfortably on hard ground.
- Any medications that you take regularly, including directions for use.
- Water filter or iodine tablets. Unless you plan to boil all your water for three minutes, you should be equipped to treat water. Because water is so heavy, you will not be able to carry enough water for more than one day of hiking.
- Camping pots, spoons, and cups. You can buy kits that will have everything you need in a compact, easy-to-pack form. Don't worry about forks; you'll be fine with spoons and your pocketknife.
- Backpacker stove and fuel. Small, single-burner stoves powered by small natural gas canisters are the easiest and most reliable.

- Cleaning supplies. Bring biodegradable soap, salt (useful as a gargle and a cleanser as well as a food seasoning), and a sponge.
- Food that is lightweight, not easily spoilable, and easy to prepare, such as dehydrated fruits and vegetables, instant oatmeal, hot cocoa, tea, flat breads, pasta, couscous, dried meats, and hard cheeses. Meal replacement or supplement bars are good as snacks but not enough to live on when backpacking.

Please be aware that there are many more items that are necessary for camping, depending on the climate of the area in which you are camping, the number of days you plan to be out, the distance you will be from civilization, how many people you will be camping with, and a great many other factors. When planning a camping trip, be sure to gather information and advice from a variety of sources and always go with at least one person who has a fair amount of camping experience.

CHAPTER 2

DISTANCE AND CLIMATE

The types of hikes you can go on are as varied as the natural environments that exist around the world. From jungles to deserts, from glaciers to coastlines, Mother Nature offers an amazing array of outdoor experiences. The four main things to think about when planning your hike include the distance you plan to cover, the climate (average weather conditions) of the area in which you will be hiking, what kind of terrain (physical features) you will be hiking on, and whether you intend to camp overnight.

While you may be limited somewhat in the kinds of places you can go because of where you live, you still have some control over the variables. In fact, it is a good idea to decide on certain details before you hit the trail. Your experience will be safer and more fun if you make preparations for your hike in advance based on these factors. Let's first talk about distance and climate.

HOW FAR TO GO

Hiking is great exercise, and if you are already an athlete, you will have no problem starting out with day hikes about 5 miles (8 km) long. If you think that you may not be in the best shape, try doing a short hike and see how that goes. Be very careful not to head out on a loop (that's a trail that begins and ends at the same place) if you're not sure how many miles long it is. You don't want to get exhausted and be out in the middle of nowhere or find yourself unable to make it back to the car before it gets dark!

There are often maps at the trailhead that will help you find a good trail to take based on how much time you have and how far you want to go.

A good idea when planning a beginner-level hike is an "out-and-back." Out-and-back means hiking out on a trail for a certain amount of time and then turning around and heading back the way you came. Since the pace at which you can walk depends on your physical condition and the terrain, the distance you can cover in an hour varies greatly. Therefore, always allow plenty of extra time to complete your hike, and always keep track of the time. Make it a point to note the time when you start hiking and the time when you stop and turn around, and estimate when you should return to

GOING TO EXTREMES

Ever thought about *extreme* hiking? Some people train for months to take on grueling physical challenges such as climbing up dangerous rocky trails or hiking in very high or low temperatures. For example, Cheryl Strayed wrote a memoir, *Wild: From Lost to Found on the Pacific Coast Trail*, about the solo hike she took from southern California to Washington after her mother died. Sarah Marquis spent three years trekking around Asia and Australia. In all, she covered about 10,000 miles (16,093 km)! She told Elizabeth Weil of the *New York Times* magazine that her expeditions are always difficult in the beginning. But then, she said, "One day you walk 12 hours, and you don't feel pain ... You become what nature needs you to be: this wild thing."

your starting point. Ideally, you should be hiking on well-marked trails with mile markers posted along the way. If there are no mile markers, there may be a map at the trailhead that indicates the distances between certain landmarks such as a stream, a giant redwood tree, or a rock outcrop. From these you can calculate how many miles per hour you are comfortable hiking.

EXPECTED WEATHER CONDITIONS

The climate of a particular area is the average course or condition of weather, including temperature, precipitation, and wind, over a certain period of time. Climates may change with the seasons, but they are predictable enough for you to prepare for your hike. You should not try to hike in extreme weather conditions (snowy or below-zero weather, extremely high altitudes, or arid, dry landscapes with little water or shelter) unless you are very experienced and outfitted with specialized outdoor survival gear.

Hiking in cold temperatures can be very dangerous. Water freezes at 32 degrees Fahrenheit (0 degrees Celsius) and you should not hike out into the wilderness in freezing conditions. You should not camp in an area with nighttime temperatures below freezing unless you are experienced and well equipped. Avoid rain, fog, and dry heat as well.

Hypothermia is a serious, and even deadly, condition that people can develop if exposed to cold temperatures. It happens when the body temperature dips below 95 degrees Fahrenheit (0 degrees Celsius). Every year people die of exposure to the elements, many

Though the Appalachian Trail is full of hikers in the summer, this section in New Hampshire is too cold and treacherous to attempt during the winter.

of them on simple day hikes in 40 to 50 degrees Fahrenheit (4 to 10 degrees Celsius) weather. To prevent hypothermia, dress in layered clothing. Adjust your layers as often as necessary to stay comfortable throughout your hike. Never let yourself become chilled or too soaked with perspiration. If temperatures are dropping, be sure to monitor yourself and others for the signs of hypothermia: chills, shivering, lethargy, lack of coordination, and irrational behavior.

If you notice these symptoms, stop and seek shelter. Remove the wet clothing and put on all of the dry clothing available. Cover the head and neck, as these are the areas where the body loses more than half of its heat. Huddle together to generate body heat. Build a fire and drink hot liquids.

Preparing for rainy or foggy conditions on a hike is crucial. Find out what the rain patterns are for the area in which you plan to hike. What have the current weather conditions been like? Weather is not totally predictable, of course, but you can get enough of an idea of what to expect to avoid danger. Pack lightweight rain gear in case of surprise showers or thick fog (both of which can soak your clothes and put you at risk for hypothermia). Wear a wide-brimmed hat to keep your head dry and to keep water out of your eyes. Pack lots of snacks and, even if you do not plan to camp, always bring matches in a water-proof container. If you get caught in a thunderstorm, take cover. To avoid light-ning, you need to get off peaks and ridges. You want to keep a low profile, so stay out of clearings, but also stay away from the tallest trees. From a sheltered place, relax and enjoy the light show!

Don't drink water from streams or rivers on the trail unless it's marked as safe for human consumption.

Extremely hot conditions can be dangerous, too, mostly because of the risks of dehydration and heat-stroke. The average active adult needs to drink three to six quarts of water per day. Hiking in desert conditions can require three gallons per day! And don't forget that in a climate like that, the only water you can count on having is the water you carry. Signs of dehydration and heatstroke include: no need to urinate; lack of perspiration; hot, dry skin; labored breathing; dizziness; nausea; and stomach or muscle cramps. If you notice symptoms of dehydration in yourself or others, get out of the sun and into the shade, rest, drink water, and if possible, bathe the skin in cool water (but don't just jump in, as that can cause shock).

CHAPTER 3

TERRAIN

T he terrain of your trail is an important element to consider when preparing for a hike. Depending on the terrain, you may have to wear different shoes and clothing. You should not attempt to hike difficult, rocky trails if you're not in good shape. Let's look into some of the various types of hiking terrain you may experience.

FLAT TERRAIN

The most familiar terrain for hikers is simply dirt. When planning a hike on a dirt trail over rolling hills, your best bet for footwear will be your most comfortable pair of sneakers, as long as they aren't too worn. You want light and sturdy footwear that won't give you blisters. Don't forget to wear a clean pair of cotton socks that allow your feet to "breathe."

As for clothes, you will want to dress in something appropriate for the weather. If it is warm out, you will, of course, be most comfortable in shorts and a T-shirt. You may want to bring along a sweatshirt if the area where you are hiking gets chilly as the sun goes down. With luck, you will be out on the trail on a fine sunny day. Who wants to go hiking in the rain, anyway? On gentle terrain like this, you can probably hike for miles and miles without getting too tired.

ROCKY TERRAIN

As you move up higher in altitude, you may find that the soft dirt trails give way to harder, rockier ground, with a lot of loose and crumbling stones. This kind of terrain, also called scrabble or skree, is usually caused by the slow movement of glaciers that melted away thousands of years ago, leaving piles of broken rocks along their ancient paths. Scrabble can be found along spectacularly beautiful alpine, or high mountain, hikes. However, hiking on it can be dangerous. If you anticipate sections of trail over loose rock, it may be a good idea to wear footgear that provides ankle support, as ankles can turn and twist when you're walking on unstable ground. It's important to wear flexible shoes because stiff shoes will make it harder to keep your balance.

Clothing requirements for this kind of terrain are similar to those for the rolling hills hike. However, at higher altitudes it is more likely that you will be exposed to colder temperatures, and you should definitely bring along a sweatshirt and consider hiking in long pants rather than shorts. Long pants will also protect your legs from cuts and scrapes should you fall on the loose rocks.

With sturdy sneakers, long pants, and layers they can take on and off, these hikers in Hatcher Pass, Alaska, are prepared for various weather conditions and terrains.

Hiking on loose ground, particularly when that loose ground is found on hillsides and slopes, is going to be more of a workout than the rolling hills hike. It will also take more concentration and physical effort to maintain your footing. Higher altitudes have thin air, which means that there is less oxygen in the air you are breathing than at lower altitudes. You may not notice it at first, but after some exercise, you may be more tired and shorter of breath than you expected. The distance you feel comfortable covering in a certain period of time will likely be shorter than on a less rigorous hike, so be careful not to get into a situation where you overextend yourself.

RIVER GORGES

River gorges are the canyons that rivers cut through the landscape. They may or may not have a river running through them year-round, since water levels can fluctuate dramatically from season to season.

The terrain of a river gorge, like the skree mountainside, is usually made up of loose, unstable rocks and can be quite steep in places. But river gorges also have giant boulders that are smooth and rounded and usually very stable and fun to climb on. The best time of year to hike in a river gorge is in high, hot summer. Why? As long as the river itself

is calm and the current is slow, with a pair of sturdy hiking sandals (old sneakers will do as well), a bathing suit, T-shirt, and plenty of sunscreen, you could make your hike part walk, part swim! Hike upstream alongside the river, and when you've gone sufficiently far and you're getting hot and dusty and ready for a swim, carefully climb down to the water level and get in the river. Keep your

These hikers are crossing the Virgin River as they explore Zion National Park in Utah.

sandals on and sit back in the water with your feet pointed downstream. This will allow you to feel your way and steer with your legs. Then let the gentle current of the river carry you slowly back downstream to where you started. You'll finish your hot, dusty hike feeling cool and refreshed!

Please note that it is not safe to swim in rivers with white water, or in rivers that are very deep or wide, and it's never safe to swim alone. Even a seemingly calm river can be rough and dangerous in certain parts, so keep an eye out for risky areas as you hike along the river, and pay attention once you are in the water. If you begin to feel the current pulling you enough to make it difficult for you to control your movements, calmly swim with the current back to solid ground and get out and walk. Try to avoid swimming against the current, as you will quickly become exhausted and will be more easily overwhelmed by the current. Be careful, and be smart!

UP AND DOWN

Most trails make steep uphill climbs easier by switchbacking, or zigzagging, gradually up the mountainside. Switchbacks make a trail longer in distance—the shortest distance between two points is always a straight line, and a switchback trail is a crazy, crooked path. However, the steepness of the climb is not as dramatic.

Of course, switchbacks or no, an uphill trail is a serious workout. You may quickly get hot, sweaty, and tired. Don't feel bad if you need to stop and rest for a minute before continuing. Be sure to drink plenty of that water you're carrying. Your shoes should be lightweight and provide good traction. Tired legs appreciate good

Bright Angel Trail, on the south rim of the Grand Canyon in Arizona, features switchbacks that make it easier for the mules to cover the steep terrain.

TREAT YOUR FEET

Feet and ankles start to swell in the middle of the day from heat as well as use. To cope with swollen feet and avoid the blisters that are caused by tight boots, start the day wearing two pairs of socks and take off one set when you stop for lunch. Your feet will feel freer and your shoes looser. Take a break mid-hike and give your hot and tired feet a cooling rub with rubbing alcohol. Another tip is to carry a little "foot kit" that includes moleskin, second skin or liquid bandage, rubbing alcohol, and toenail clippers.

ankle support, so check out a pair of lightweight hiking boots. When choosing clothing, think layers. You want to be able to strip down to the minimum amount of clothing as you get hot and sweaty puffing up that hill. But don't forget to tie a sweatshirt around your waist. You'll need it later.

One important rule of hiking is that if you go up, you've also got to come down. It may seem tiring to hike uphill, but hiking back down a steep hill is also very strenuous and can be really hard on your feet and knees. Gravity can work against you as your tired feet pound against hard ground. Your toes may jam into the tips of your shoes, and the balls of your feet may chafe against your insoles. The last leg of your hike can be unpleasant if you're not prepared for this terrain. When going down a steep slope, try making your own little switchbacks along the trail by walking with your feet pointed to one side or the other and not straight down the mountain. Walk to the left for a few steps and then turn to the right and walk that way, making gradual progress down the hill as you go. This will save your toes and help you keep your balance on the steep slope.

Sneakers that may have seemed comfortable on the way up might not be sturdy enough or provide sufficient traction on the way down the mountain. Try not to attempt terrain like this in shoes that have not yet been broken in.

You may find that you begin to get a little chilly as you start heading downhill. Your muscles produce more heat during the aerobic exercise of carrying your weight up the mountain. Even though you may be moving faster on the way down, you are not getting the same workout. The sweat from the uphill climb may start to chill you a little. This is the time to put on the sweatshirt that you have tied around your waist. And you thought you would never need it!

CHAPTER 4

STAYING SAFE

Even on a well-marked trail, you could run into trouble. When planning a hike or thinking about spending time outdoors, safety is something that should always be in the back of your mind. If you plan ahead and educate yourself as much as you can, you will be able to enjoy your outdoor recreation much more.

Above all, the most important safety precaution to take when going hiking is never to go on a long hike alone. Many experienced hikers do enjoy being out in the wilderness alone, but as a beginner, it is not recommended. If you are on a family or scouting camping trip and decide to spend a day by yourself exploring the woods, be very sure that someone, preferably a responsible adult, knows what time you left, what time you will be back, and where, in general, you are planning to hike.

MOUNTAIN LIONS AND BEARS

While hiking in North America, there is a strong possibility that you may encounter bears, mountain lions, and all sorts of other creatures. Don't forget that seeing wildlife in its natural habitat is above all an exciting and beautiful thing. There's no need to be afraid of an animal sighting, but you should definitely be prepared, starting with reading up on the area where you'll be hiking.

Big Bend National Park in Texas posts signs to warn hikers about how to keep bears away and what to do if they come across one.

Bear Country

When Hiking
- Never Leave Packs or Food Unattended
- Avoid Carrying Odorous Food or Toiletry Items
- Carry Out Trash and Left-Over Food

If You See a Bear
- Keep a Safe Distance
- If a Bear Approaches, Scare it Away
  - Shout, Wave Arms, Throw Stones
- Never Feed or Approach a Bear
- Report All Bear Sightings to a Ranger

Removal of this sign is illegal and endangers others

Ask a ranger what the bear and mountain lion conditions are in the area. The National Parks Service tracks large predators, so the ranger should be able to tell you quite accurately how many animals are in the area and even what the behavior of these animals is. For example, have mountain lions frequently been spotted near high human-traffic areas such as trails? Have bears been seen raiding campsites?

Bears are a problem mainly for campers who are carrying a lot of food and who are cooking outdoors. The smell of cooked food can attract a bear to the campsite, but occasionally bears can be a danger to hikers, too. Be particularly alert for bear cubs. They are cute and cuddly-looking, but they are never far from a ferocious and very protective mother who doesn't want you anywhere near her babies. If you see a cub or a full-grown bear, the best thing to do is to calmly move away from the area, keeping as great a distance as possible from the animal. But don't stray far from the trail! You wouldn't want to get away from the bear and then not know how to get back.

Mountain lions are endangered animals that are beginning to make a comeback in some areas of the United States. They are normally very shy of people and, unlike bears, are uninterested in stealing your food. If you see a mountain lion, the standard advice is to appear large, loud, and unafraid. Don't be aggressive toward the animal, but don't run away. The message you want to send to a mountain lion is that people are not prey. That is not as hard as it might seem, since it's true. Mountain lions have a variety of natural prey, including deer, squirrels, and rabbits, and humans are not one of them.

SNAKES

Luckily, most North American snakes are not poisonous, but it's a good idea to check which species of snakes are native to your area. Most snakes are insectivores and are very important parts of the food chain. That's why you should never kill a snake! Usually snakes, even the poisonous ones, are docile toward humans, although people often are irrationally afraid of them. To avoid unwanted snake encounters, don't put your hands or feet where you cannot see them, such as inside rock crevices or in thick brush. Snakes will bite a person if stepped on, startled, or threatened. Another tip is to

The venomous western diamondback rattlesnake is found in northern Mexico and the southwest United States.

walk with a walking stick. The extra thump of the stick hitting the ground will send vibrations through the earth that nearby snakes can feel, warning them that people are passing through and to get out of the way.

If you get bitten by a North American venomous snake, such as a rattlesnake or a moccasin, the best thing to do is to stay quiet and comfortable and to get medical attention immediately. You can also carry a snakebite kit, which will give you further instructions and may even contain a small dose of venom antidote.

TICKS

Ticks are small parasitic arachnids that attach themselves to humans and feed on blood. They can also carry very serious diseases, such as Lyme disease and Rocky Mountain spotted fever. Ticks wait in trees and shrubs and grab on to people as they brush past. They seek out the most tender spots to bite, so check yourself periodically for ticks, focusing on your groin area, behind your knees, on your neck, and in your armpits. Check frequently when hiking in dense vegetation and try using

JOHN MUIR

John Muir, one of America's most important conservationists, was born in Scotland in 1838 and immigrated with his family to Wisconsin when he was nine years old. At age twenty-nine, Muir left his job in Indianapolis and began his years of wandering the country. He walked 1,000 miles (1,609 km) from Indiana to the Gulf of Mexico, eventually ending up in California, where, though he would continue to travel the world, he made his home. The Sierra Nevada, and in particular the spectacular Yosemite Valley, were the areas closest to Muir's heart. In 1874 he published the first of a series of articles entitled "Studies in the Sierra" that launched his career as a successful writer.

During his lifetime, he traveled to Alaska, Australia, South America, Africa, Europe, China, and Japan and published three hundred articles and ten books on his travels and his naturalist philosophy. He urged everyone to "climb the mountains and get their good tidings." Often called the father of our national park system, Muir helped to establish Yosemite, Sequoia, Mount Rainier, Petrified Forest, and Grand Canyon national parks. In 1892 Muir founded the Sierra Club, one of America's most influential conservationist and environmental organizations, to "do something for wildness and make the mountains glad."

Thanks to the dedication of John Muir and the Sierra Club, Americans have many protected wilderness areas to explore and enjoy. Through his writings, he has taught generations of people the importance of experiencing and preserving our natural heritage.

insect repellent on your clothes to discourage hitchhiking ticks from sticking around.

If you are bitten by a tick, remove the entire tick by using rubbing alcohol or petroleum jelly to smother it. This will either kill the tick or cause it to let go and back out. If you remove the tick, but the head remains embedded in your skin, go to the doctor.

POISON IVY, POISON OAK, AND SUMAC

These plants produce resins on their leaves and branches that cause itchy rashes and, depending on how severely allergic you are, seriously debilitating reactions. Learn which of these plants you are most likely to encounter on your hike and how to identify them. If you think you may have touched one, try not to spread the resin around. Avoid touching your face and other parts of your body with hands that have touched the exposed area. Wash the area with water, but do not use soap, which helps to spread it. If you can, change out of the clothing you suspect might have touched the plant. If you develop a reaction, which appears as a red, bumpy, spreading rash, use calamine lotion to soothe the itching. An antihistamine, which helps to block the body's allergic reactions, also may be helpful.

Like poison ivy, poison oak can be identified by its three-leaf structure. It is found on both coasts in North America, whereas poison ivy is common across the continent.

GETTING LOST

The prospect of getting lost in the woods may be scary, but if you are prepared and have a plan for how to get back to your starting point and the rest of your group, you'll have nothing to fear. While hiking, pay constant attention to landmarks along the trail. Make mental and even written notes of features and the order in which you see them as you hike, so that if you need to turn and go back, you can recognize where you are and have a ballpark idea of how far you need to go. Be suspicious if a very clear trail suddenly becomes very faint; you may have taken a wrong turn without realizing it. Always remain calm if you become lost. Stop walking until you reorient yourself.

Then, use the map and compass you've been carrying to figure out where you are. Most of the time you will use a topographical, or "topo," map for deep wilderness areas, which shows natural landmarks such as hills, peaks, valleys, and bodies of water where there are no roads to reference. These maps work differently from the way street maps do, so be sure you know how to read a topo map before you head out. Landmarks on the map may not be visible on the ground or may look quite different from what you expect.

Be sure you know how to read the compass and which direction you'll need to head in to get back to home base. Don't forget that a compass is only useful if you already have your orientation. You have to know where you are to get to where you want to go. The rule is to always know where you are, in what direction you have been hiking, and for how long. Locating yourself from a completely unknown position, even with a map and compass, is not easy.

If you are hiking with a group, be sure to establish a meeting place along the trail or at home base if you become separated. Make sure that everyone in the group is very clear about the plan. Another useful thing to have in case you become separated from your hiking companions is a whistle. The shrill sound is distinctive and will carry for some distance. Only blow the whistle in emergencies. One blast of the whistle every thirty seconds or so will help your party to locate you. Three blasts in a row is the universal call for help.

CHAPTER 5

HIKING TRADITIONS AND CLUBS

Hiking is part of a long tradition, seen in many cultures around the world, of experiencing and respecting the natural environment. This tradition is carried on by many organizations that plan outdoor activities for young people, such as the Boy Scouts, Girl Scouts, and Outward Bound.

NATIVE RELIGIONS

Nature-focused religions regard the earth and the plants and animals that live on it as equal to humans in their importance. People do not own the land, but belong to it, in a partnership with other living things. In many Native American religions, animals such as the crow and the coyote are believed to have great wisdom and lessons to teach to humans. Many different Native American cultures have rites of passage in which young people venture out alone into

Uluru is a sacred location to Aborigines. Also known as Ayers Rock, it is located in central Australia and is about seven hundred million years old.

the wilderness, hiking far from camp and spending many nights in isolation to gain wisdom and courage from the experience.

The native people of Australia, known as Aborigines (the word "Aborigine" means "from the beginning"), have a hiking tradition of their own that is also deeply rooted in a spiritual connection to the earth. The European colonists who settled in Australia coined the term "walkabout" to refer to the Aborigines' roaming way of life. To the Europeans, who believed in having fixed, permanent homes, the partly nomadic lifestyle of the native Australians seemed to stem from a compulsive, or uncontrollable, urge to travel about the land. The truth is that the Australian Aborigines have very complex religious and practical ties to the landscape and have connections to many different sites spread across the land for hundreds of miles. An individual may spend his or her life "on walkabout," traveling to various sites of spiritual importance and making a living from the land along the way.

SCOUTING

Getting outdoors and into nature, whether it's a wilderness area far from civilization or a recreation area just outside of town, can be an uplifting experience. Sometimes it can be a challenge, though. For those who live in big cities, it may be difficult to get out of the urban environment. Anyone without a driver's license and a car may find transportation unavailable or inaccessible. It may be hard for young people to organize a group that includes adult supervision.

Luckily, scouting groups such as the Boy Scouts and Girl Scouts help kids all over the country to participate in outdoor activities in

These boys and girls are participating in an international scouting camp in Almke, Germany.

natural environments. These organizations don't just help young people take a trip to the country. They also teach them important things about cooperation, community, and facing challenges. Besides these well-known organizations, there are many other national and local groups you may find in your area.

Most scouting groups have a similar mission and work in similar ways. Their basic philosophy is that by spending time in the wilderness, young people can learn important skills and lessons that they wouldn't be able to learn in a classroom. Scout troops are clubs for boys and girls that teach a variety of different activities, but they place a special emphasis on the outdoors and community service.

JULIETTE GORDON LOW

Born to a wealthy family in Savannah, Georgia, in 1860, Juliette Gordon Low, or "Daisy" as she was called, was in her fifties when she began the work for which she is remembered. In 1912, she dreamed of starting something in America that would be "for all the girls." She envisioned an organization that would help bring girls out of their sheltered and stifling home environments into the world to experience the outdoors and serve in their communities. Before women had even won the right to vote in the United States, Low founded the Girl Scouts of America. Soon groups of young girls were hiking through the woods, playing basketball, going camping together, and learning first-aid and outdoor cooking techniques— all activities that were seen as foolish and improper for girls during that time.

In all, fifty-nine million women have participated in Girl Scouts since it was founded over one hundred years ago. Today the Girl Scouts continue Juliette Gordon Low's mission with various health, fitness, and sports projects for girls and young women across the country, as well as service projects. The youngest Girl Scouts, kindergarteners and first-graders, are known as Daisy Scouts after Low's nickname.

If you live in a city or suburb and are a member of a scouting club, you may not go hiking every day, but you will probably participate in a few camping trips throughout the year. You will learn things about camping and hiking safety from your scout leader, and you will have his or her help in organizing trips. You will make friends with other scouts in your troop and have people your age with whom to share outdoor adventures. In addition, you will participate in projects designed to help your community. Depending on where you live, these projects could be anything from reading to the elderly or cleaning up city lots and making gardens to starting recycling programs. Often it is up to the scouts themselves to decide on what kinds of projects their troop will work.

OUTWARD BOUND

Outward Bound is another outdoors organization designed especially for young people, although now it also has programs for adults. Unlike the scouting groups, Outward Bound is not a club. It's more like a wilderness school. The idea of a school may not sound like much fun, but this is a different kind of learning experience. The hiking philosophy of the Outward Bound organization can be summed up by their three core principles: learning through experience, challenge and adventure, and supportive environment. The goal is for students to demonstrate their character development, leadership, and service. Many of the guidelines for campers, hikers, and backpackers recommended by the U.S. Forest Service and National Park Service originated in Outward Bound instructors' manuals.

On an Outward Bound course, groups of six to twelve people (that's four to ten students plus one instructor and one assistant) are in the wilderness for a certain number of days. By facing different outdoor challenges as a team, students learn about themselves as well as how to reach out and help other members of the team.

In this Outward Bound challenge, the woman on the left is leading her blindfolded partner up the hill without communicating verbally.

In addition to these lessons, Outward Bound courses teach cutting-edge techniques on backcountry survival, including the environmental philosophy of "leave no trace." This practice involves living a simple, self-reliant, low-impact lifestyle in the wilderness. The goal is to reap the rewards and benefits of nature while at the same time leaving behind no evidence that you have been there—especially no trash! Another expression is "Take nothing but pictures; leave nothing but footprints."

Aside from Outward Bound, there are many local organizations such as the Youth Enrichment Services Outdoor Adventure Program in New England and Seattle Inner-City Outings in Washington State. These groups help youths from urban areas who would not otherwise be able to take trips to wilderness areas. Their philosophy is that no matter where you live or how much money you have, you should be able to enjoy the richness and tranquility of the outdoors.

CHAPTER 6

OTHER HIKING ACTIVITIES

you may think hiking is only good for exercising and getting away from the stress of everyday life. Maybe the idea of walking around in nature even sounds a little dull. But there are a bunch of different fun activities you can incorporate into your hike, too. Here are just a few suggestions.

BIRD-WATCHING AND MORE

Pick up a book at your local library or bookstore about the plants and animals of the area where you will be hiking. Many different guidebooks are available that are small enough to carry easily in your backpack. They are are full of beautiful color illustrations and photos that can help you to identify wildflowers, trees, other native plants, birds, mammals, reptiles, and even insects. Your natural heritage will be so much more precious to you when you take

These bird watchers are observing white-winged crossbills in Glacier National Park in Montana.

notice of the diversity of life around you. So many different plants and creatures call the wilderness their home—it is important that we preserve and appreciate it.

FASCINATING HISTORY

Many national parks and trails played important and fascinating roles in the history of this country. Just by doing a little research at the library or online, you can discover amazing things about an area. Maybe the region of your hike was once the home of Native Americans who left things such as arrowheads, paintings, or carv-

GEOCACHING

Geocaching is an outdoor game akin to treasure hunting or scavenger hunting. Participants use Global Positioning Systems (GPS) to hide and seek waterproof containers, or "caches." Often they contain assorted objects, or "treasures," such as collectible coins or small toys. Anything dangerous, illegal, or perishable (such as food) is not allowed. There is also a logbook where participants record the date that they discovered the cache.

Most geocachers say the fun is in the exploration of the world around them, not what treasures they may find. As geocacher Billy Easterbrooks told WACH Fox News in Columbia, South Carolina, "We joke about how we use billion dollar satellites to find Tupperware containers in the woods." Usually, geocachers will take only one object from the stash and perhaps leave another for the next person to find. With some items, called trackables, geocachers will keep moving them around to different caches and record their movement online.

Geocaching only became possible in 2000, after GPS became available to the general public. Now, ten million people all around the world participate in geocaching using smartphones or other devices with GPS capability. You can get a list of cache locations at websites such as http://www.geocaching.com.

ings on stone, mortar holes in the bedrock, or other physical evidence of their lives. Find out more. Who were these people? How did they live? When and why did they move from this place? Are there any remaining members of the tribe living nearby?

You may be hiking on an old immigrant trail used by settlers from the East seeking new lives in the West. Where were they from? When did this happen? What was the cross-country journey like? Where did they eventually settle? You could be hiking trails used by Native Americans, trappers, missionaries, conquistadors, naturalists, stagecoaches, miners, lumberjacks, and outlaws. Explore the history of your wilderness areas. You may even learn something about your own family's history in the process!

SELF-REFLECTION

You can learn a lot about yourself by spending time in the wilderness. Sometimes the trappings of our lives and the details of our daily routines get in the way of who we really are. When you're planning your hike with your companions, you may want to agree ahead of time to make a stop along the way where each of you can take a little time out from the group. Go sit on a rock on your own, a little distance from the others. You may find that, in quiet moments, you begin to forget about the worries that plague you. You gain a new perspective on things. Try bringing your journal or diary with you. If you don't already have one, this may be a good time to start keeping one.

Many people find great inspiration in the solitude. You may want to bring a camera, sketchbook, or watercolor set so you

Hiking can lead you to spectacular, breathtaking views, such as this one from the Haiku Stairs, or Stairway to Heaven, on the island of Oahu in Hawaii.

can capture the beauty all around you. Express your thoughts and your feelings creatively. Close your eyes for a moment and listen to the sounds of nature around you. Take a deep breath and smell the freshness and fullness of the air. Then open your eyes again. Try looking at things in a new way.

55

GLOSSARY

ALTITUDE The height, or vertical elevation, above a surface, usually measured in feet or meters above sea level.

ANTIHISTAMINE A drug that is used to treat allergies by blocking the physiological effects of histamine, a crystalline base that is released during allergic reactions.

ARID Very dry; usually used to describe areas that don't receive enough rainfall for crops to grow.

BACTERIA Single-celled microrganisms. Some are beneficial to human beings, and some cause a variety of diseases.

BIODEGRADABLE Able to be decomposed by the action of microorganisms or other living things.

CLIMATE The general pattern of weather for a particular geographical area as measured over a certain length of time, such as a season, a year, or longer.

CONSERVATIONIST A person who believes in preserving the natural environment.

DEHYDRATION A severe loss of bodily fluids, which can be fatal.

FOOD CHAIN An arrangement of organisms in which each is a predator dependent on another species to be its source of food.

HYPOTHERMIA A dangerous, potentially fatal reduction in body temperature caused by exposure to the cold.

OUTCROP A visible rock formation.

POTABLE Safe for drinking.

RITE OF PASSAGE A cultural ceremony that celebrates a certain stage of life, such as becoming an adult.

SCRABBLE A type of rocky, loose terrain often created by the movement of glaciers.

SELF-RELIANT Independent; able to depend on one's own capabilities instead of other people's.

SPECIES A class or group of living organisms having certain common features and being capable of reproducing.

SWITCHBACK A trail that zigzags up a steep slope so that the change in altitude is more gradual for the hiker.

TERRAIN The physical features of an area of land.

TOPOGRAPHICAL The representation of geographical features in graphic (drawn or printed) form, such as a topographical map.

TRAILHEAD The point at which a trail begins.

TRANSCENDENTALISM A social and philosophical movement, started in the 1830s in New England, that believed in the divinity of all nature and humanity.

FOR MORE INFORMATION

Appalachian Trail Conservancy
799 Washington Street
P.O. Box 807
Harpers Ferry, WV 25425-0807
(304) 535-6331
Website: http://www.appalachiantrail.org
The Appalachian Trail Conservancy is a nonprofit organization that maintains and preserves the Appalachian Trail. It also sponsors youth, education, and community programs.

Boy Scouts of America
Empire State Building, #530 Fifth Avenue
New York, NY 10118
(212) 242-1100
Website: http://www.scouting.org
The Boy Scouts of America has served over 114 million youth since its founding in 1910. Scouts earn merit badges, volunteer in their communities, and stay fit through outdoor recreation.

Girl Scouts
420 Fifth Avenue
New York, NY 10018-2798
(800) 478-7248
Website: http://www.girlscouts.org
Over fifty-nine million young women have participated in Girl Scouts since 1912. They participate in and organize community service projects, earn awards and merit badges, and often go on field trips, including hiking and camping trips.

Hike Ontario
262 Lavender Drive
Ancaster, ON L9K 1E5
Canada
(800) 894-7249

Website: http://www.hikecanada.org/en
Hike Ontario is one of the provincial associations of Hike Canada, an organization founded in 1971 with the goal of establishing a hiking foot trail that covers Canada from coast to coast.

Outward Bound
910 Jackson Street, Suite 140
Golden, CO 80401
(866) 467-7651
Website: http://www.outwardbound.org
Outward Bound sponsors outdoor expeditions that teach leadership skills and strength of character to people of all ages and backgrounds, including struggling teens and those with health, social, or educational challenges.

Parks Canada
30 Victoria Street
Gatineau, QC J8X 0B3
Canada
(888) 773-8888
Website: http://www.pc.gc.ca/eng/index.aspx
Parks Canada is responsible for protecting Canada's many diverse national parks. It also administers some of Canada's national historic sites, maintains national marine conservation areas, and is committed to ecological integrity and the conservation of endangered species.

The Sierra Club
85 Second Street, 2nd Floor
San Francisco, CA 94105
(415) 977-5500
Website: http://www.sierraclub.org
Sierra Club, the environmental group founded by John Muir in 1892, has sixty-four local chapters across the United States. In addition to sponsoring outings around the world that are suitable for people of all ages and skill levels, Sierra Club is committed to protecting the wilderness and moving toward a clean energy economy.

Walden Pond State Reservation
915 Walden Street
Concord, MA 01742
(978) 369-3254
Website: http://www.nps.gov/nr/travel/massachusetts_conservation/
walden_pond.html
Walden Pond, where Henry David Thoreau famously lived for two years to escape
the busyness of city life, is now a National Historic Landmark and part of a Massachusetts state reservation. Visitors can enjoy all kinds of outdoor activities at Walden
Pond, including hiking, swimming, boating, and skiing.

WEBSITES

Because of the changing nature of Internet links, Rosen Publishing has developed
an online list of websites related to the subject of this book. This site is updated regularly. Please use this link to access the list:

http://www.rosenlinks.com/OUT/Hike

FOR FURTHER READING

Lichter, Justin. *Trail Tested: A Thru-Hiker's Guide to Ultralight Hiking and Backpacking.* Guilford, CT: Falcon Guides, 2013.

Miller, David. *AWOL on the Appalachian Trail.* New York, NY: Mariner Books, 2011.

Muir, John. *Nature Writings.* New York, NY: Library of America, 1997.

Potterfield, Peter. *Classic Hikes of North America: 25 Breathtaking Treks in the United States and Canada.* New York, NY: W.W. Norton, 2012.

Randall, Glenn. *Outward Bound Map & Compass Handbook.* Guilford, CT: Falcon Guides, 2012.

Skurka, Andrew. *The Ultimate Hiker's Gear Guide.* Washington, DC: National Geographic, 2012.

Strayed, Cheryl. *Wild: From Lost to Found on the Pacific Crest Trail.* New York, NY: Vintage Books, 2013.

Thoreau, Henry David. *Walden and Civil Disobedience.* New York, NY: Signet Classics, 2012.

Townsend, Chris. *The Backpacker's Handbook.* 4th ed. New York, NY: McGraw Hill, 2012.

Wenk, Elizabeth. *John Muir Trail: The Essential Guide to Hiking America's Most Famous Trail.* 5th ed. Birmingham, AL: Wilderness Press, 2014.

INDEX

ABOUT THE AUTHORS

Amy Beattie is a writer from New Hampshire. A former Outward Bound instructor, she enjoys hiking in the White Mountains with her Scottish terrier.

Sara Coppin grew up in northern California, where she hiked in the Sierra Nevada mountains, read banned books, and listened to punk music because there wasn't much else to do.

PHOTO CREDITS

Cover, p. 1 Daxiao Productions/Shuitterstock.com; p. 5 Gareth Mccormack/Lonely Planet Images/Getty Images; pp. 7, 17 Hero Images/Getty Images; p. 9 Yellow Dog Productions/The Image Bank/Getty Images; pp. 10-11 Paul Rocheleau/Photolibrary/Getty Images; p. 13 Oleh Slobodeniuk/E+/Getty Images; p. 20 MyLoupe/Universal Images Group/Getty Images; p. 21 Jose Azel/Getty Images; pp. 24-25 Bread and Butter Productions/The Image Bank/Getty Images; pp. 26-27 Karen Crowe/All Canada Photos/Getty Images; p. 29 Justin Locke/National Geographic Image Collection/Getty Images; p. 33 © Chris Howes/Wild Places Photography/Alamy; p. 35 Ryan M. Bolton/Shutterstock.com; p. 39 Dwight Smith/iStock/Thinkstock; p. 43 David Wall Photo/Lonely Planet Images/Getty Images; p. 45 Andreas Rentz/Getty Images; pp. 48-49 Hyoung Chang/The Denver Post/Getty Images; p. 51 © AP Images; pp. 54-55 Laszlo Podor/Moment/Getty Images; cover and interior pages Iwona Grodzka/iStock/Thinkstock (twig frame), AKIRA/amanaimagesRF/Thinkstock (wood frame)

Designer: Brian Garvey; Editor: Meredith Day
Photo Researcher: Karen Huang